THOMAS CRANE PUBLIC LIBRARY
QUINCY MA

CITY APPROPRIATION

# PLANET SOS
# FARMING
# FOR THE FUTURE

## Gerry Bailey

 **Gareth Stevens**
Publishing

**Please visit our Web site, www.garethstevens.com. For a free color catalog of all our high-quality books, call toll free 1-800-542-2595 or fax 1-877-542-2596.**

Library of Congress Cataloging-in-Publication Data

Bailey, Gerry.
  Farming for the future / Gerry Bailey.
      p. cm. — (Planet SOS)
  Includes index.
  ISBN 978-1-4339-4966-1 (library binding)
  ISBN 978-1-4339-4967-8 (pbk.)
  ISBN 978-1-4339-4968-5 (6-pack)
1.  Agriculture—Juvenile literature 2.  Food supply—Juvenile literature.  I. Title. II. Series: Planet SOS.
  S519.B245 2011
  630—dc22

                                2010032887

Published in 2011 by
**Gareth Stevens Publishing**
111 East 14th Street, Suite 349
New York, NY 10003

Designer: Simon Webb
Editor: Felicia Law

Printed in the United States of America

CPSIA compliance information: Batch #CW11GS: For further information contact Gareth Stevens, New York, New York at 1-800-542-2595.

# CONTENTS

# FROM THE SOIL

Soil is almost everywhere – at least on the land. In fact, most of the land on our planet is covered in a layer of soil. Without soil, animals couldn't live and we couldn't easily grow trees, flowers, or food crops.

Knowing what different types of soil are made of helps scientists to know how quickly water will move through it and whether or not the soil will be good for growing crops.

Soil is a combination of two different kinds of material. One kind includes air, water, tiny living things, and bits of rotting plants and animals. That's the top layer. The other kind, the lower layer, is made up of tiny pieces of rock.

*Soil is made up of different layers.*

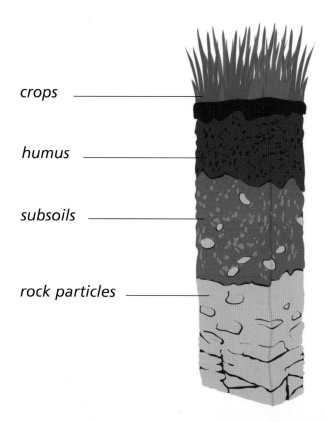

crops

humus

subsoils

rock particles

*Plants root and grow in the shallow layer of topsoil. Roots draw in nutrients such as water and minerals.*

## Humus

The "organic" part – the part made up of formerly living things – is called humus. It is mostly made up of the leaves, stems, and flowers of dead plants. Tiny animals living in the soil (such as bacteria and molds) and invertebrates (such as insects and worms) feed on the dead plant material. The waste that they leave is full of nutrients and minerals, which are needed by living plants to grow. Humus also helps to keep the air warm (which helps seeds germinate faster) and to hold water in the soil.

The rest of the soil is made up of rock, sand, and clay. Most of it is not alive and never has been, so we say it is "inorganic."

*Soil that is good for crops is rich in humus.*

## Ever-changing soil

Soil develops over hundreds of thousands of years, but as Earth's surface is constantly changing, the different layers and kinds of soil are constantly changing too. Changes in the climate, even extreme ones, will play a part. The arrival of new kinds of plant and animal life also makes a difference. Lastly, changes to the shape of the land, such as those caused by volcanic eruptions, will change and move soil and rock around.

*Without roots to hold it in place, exposed soil cracks and is blown away.*

*Goats and sheep nibble plants down to the roots. The plants soon die.*

# Looking after the soil

Soil takes many years to turn into a rich and nutritious material for growing crops and forage. It can take 500 years for a depth of just 0.6 inches (1.5 cm) of soil to develop naturally. Around 6 inches (15 cm) is needed to grow good crops.

Soil disappears for many reasons. The process is called erosion, and it describes what happens when soil or rock is worn away by the wind or rain. Land that is now desert has not always been empty, dry, and barren. The reason many deserts now exist is because the land was overgrazed by farm animals. If the land is overgrazed it is no longer held together by plant roots and erodes more easily.

*When soil is eroded, tree roots are exposed and die.*

*Tree roots bind the soil together.*

# Keeping the soil in place

Trees protect the landscape from erosion by holding the soil together. Their roots dig deep into the ground and the soil clings to them. The land around trees fills with leaves, broken twigs, and branches and these also help to bind the soil.

Poor farming methods can exhaust and erode topsoil in just 30 years, and it then takes 3,000 years to get it back naturally.

crown

roots

*The roots of a tree stretch out below the soil to the same extent that the crown of the tree does above.*

# Great green walls

Deserts are expanding in many parts of the world. Once land is empty of plants, perhaps due to overgrazing or poor water management, the wind can blow the dusty surface away and spread it further. Once a piece of land is dry, the air above it is drier too: rainfall is reduced, so the land gets drier still. This process is called "desertification."

## Reducing pollution in China

The Gobi Desert covers more than 380,000 sq miles (a million sq km) in China. And it's growing as a result of the causes that create most deserts — deforestation, overgrazing, and the extraction of its natural water resources.

Every spring the sky over Beijing in China and over Seoul in neighboring South Korea is darkened by huge sandstorms that pollute the atmosphere. Chinese scientists calculate that until recently, almost 4,000 miles (10,000 sq km) of arable land was lost to desert every year. China's response has been to create the largest planting program in history, a "Great Green Wall" of trees, stretching 2,783 miles (4,480 km) to protect farms and cities from floods and the desert.

*Sand moves across the land, burying trees as it goes.*

## More farmland in Africa

There is a similar plan in Africa. In many Central and West African countries bordering the huge Sahara Desert, rainfall has slowed to a trickle, crops have died, and soil has been eroded. If this continues, scientists forecast that two-thirds of Africa's farmland may be swallowed by sand by 2025.

The project involves planting trees over a distance of 4,349 miles (7,000 km) from Dakar on the Atlantic coast to Djibouti on the Indian Ocean. This will make a green strip 3 miles (5 km) wide across the desert and stop further desertification.

*The Great Green Wall of Africa*

# FEED THE WORLD

Scientists and farmers are always looking for ways to help feed the growing population of the world. Fifty years ago there were food shortages and severe difficulties in various parts of the world. An American biologist, Paul R. Ehrlich, made worrying statements and predicted global famine in the 1970s and 1980s. People also remembered the words of an English writer, Thomas Malthus, who 200 years before had made predictions about how the world was going to run out of food.

*In Vietnam, rice production doubled in the Green Revolution.*

*When emergencies occur throughout the world, it is usually possible to get food to hungry people quickly.*

## The Green Revolution

Fortunately, these predictions proved to be wrong. Instead, there were a number of developments in agriculture, which together came to be known as the Green Revolution. Scientists developed new fertilizers and found ways to breed better varieties of wheat and rice. They also introduced new methods of irrigation and better farm implements. Over the next 20 years, they succeeded in developing crops that were shorter in height and had larger seeds. These produced up to three times more grain than traditional varieties.

*The use of fertilizers and new kinds of seeds increased production in India.*

## The hidden cost of food

There is no doubt that these increases in agricultural productivity have brought about one of the greatest achievements of modern civilization – the elimination of food scarcity in much of the world. There's no way that human numbers could have risen as dramatically as they have without them. Yet the hidden costs of this success story are soil erosion, chemical pollution, and unsustainable water consumption.

# The "carbon cost" of food

It is a sad fact that in order to have bigger farm machines, more oil-based chemicals and fertilizers, and more packaged and processed food, we are not helping the planet. Today, food manufacturing is almost 100 percent dependent on the use of fossil fuels (such as oil and coal). And all of this means creating a bigger and bigger "carbon footprint" – pouring more and more fuel emissions into the atmosphere and making global warming an ever bigger problem.

## Growing meat

In some countries, meat is an everyday food; in other countries it's a rare luxury. Yet an increasing number of people want to eat meat in their diet and farmers have responded by increasing their herds. A new study from scientists in Japan has

*Large herds of cattle give off methane, a powerful greenhouse gas.*

calculated that 2.2 pounds (1 kg) of beef is responsible for giving off the same amount of destructive carbon dixide as an average car driving more than 150 miles (240 km).

## Losing fish

Fish is a healthy source of protein, and many people eat it as an alternative to meat, or are finding new ways to make it part of their diet. As a result, consumption of seafood is twice as high as it was 40 years ago.

Industrial fishing methods damage the oceans' ecosystems, and have damaged fish levels so badly that scientists predict that at this rate, all commercially fished wild seafood will be wiped out by 2050 – unless we change our ways.

*Fish on sale at a market in Thailand.*

## Buy local!

Many stores are buying more goods from local farmers to reduce the cost of transport. They are also stocking more organic foods and fewer that use expensive and scarce fossil fuels in their production.

*There are low transport costs if farmers sell produce from local stalls and shops.*

# GM crops

For thousands of years, farmers and scientists have practiced selective breeding of plants and animals, slowly changing aspects of them to make them better. But now, scientists can alter living things much faster and in a new way – at the level of the cells themselves, in a process called genetic modification (GM).

GM involves changing the genes in a plant or animal. Genes are tiny parts of the cells of every living thing that map out exactly what kind of thing it is – what kind of plant, its color, and so on. When scientists modify the genetic structure of a plant, they change what kind of plant it is.

## Hit or miss?

When scientists try to create a "better" kind of plant, they put a new gene, or group of genes, into it. The aim is to create plants that, for example, grow faster, produce larger yields or are more resistant to drought.

But many people believe that genetic changes could produce foods that are bad for humans and other animals to eat. They might also contaminate other plant crops, or even the whole environment. No one really knows.

*These GM wheat and corn crops are strong and have full seeds.*

# We're watching!

Greenpeace is an organization that works to protect the environment. It will try to expose the amount of secret GM corn-growing that is taking place. It also aims to discover if genetically modified maize is bad for the environment and in what ways.

*Greenpeace campaigns against GM crops by creating messages in the fields.*

# Growing crops

Successfully growing crops depends on three things – the seeds, the soil, and what goes into the soil, such as water and nutrients. There are 50,000 different kinds of soil on our planet. Some of these are especially good for agriculture, or growing crops. Crops are usually grown in topsoil – the uppermost layer of the soil. This is the richest part because it contains the most humus and can take hundreds of years to build up.

As the roots draw in all the nutrients, such as water and minerals, the topsoil needs to be continually enriched with more nutrients. There are different ways to do this, from using man-made fertilizer, which is made of chemical compounds, to spreading well-rotted manure or compost on the fields.

*Sunflowers are grown for the oil in their seeds, making them a valuable cash crop.*

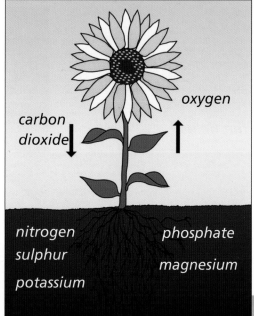

## What are nutrients?

Plant nutrients are chemical elements needed by plants for growth. The most common elements in plants are carbon, hydrogen, and oxygen, obtained from air and water. All other nutrients are available in soil. Six of these are important: calcium, magnesium, nitrogen, phosphorus, potassium, and sulphur.

*Crops flourish on soil that is full of nutrients.*

## Natural or organic fertilizers

Manure is animal dung. Compost is rotted-down plant matter. And they're both packed with important nutrients. Farmers can also enrich their soils by growing certain crops that put essential nitrogen into the soil, such as soybeans.

## Chemical fertilizers

Man-made fertilizers contain all the mineral nutrients normally found in soil. They are plowed into the soil before the crop is sown, or sprayed over the fields where huge areas need to be treated.

*Compost and manure are rich in natural nutrients.*

# Organic farming

Organic farming is a method of sustainable agriculture. It can be practiced without wearing out the soil, killing off all the animals in the earth, or polluting the water around it. It involves using organic fertilizers and compost, and avoiding the use of poisonous chemicals.

Compost is made by collecting dead plants in a heap and allowing them to decay, or rot, into a soft, soil-like mixture. Crops fertilized with compost are bigger and healthier, while the compost helps the soil develop much quicker than it would naturally. This is one good way to build up soil that has been lost through erosion.

## Helping the soil

Regenerating the soil not only helps farmers, it also helps the survival of many plants and animals that keep the soil fertile. Worm tunnels help soil absorb water faster and allow air to get down deeper. As they eat their way through the dead plant material on top of the soil, worms pass the nutrients through their bodies and lower down into the soil.

*Worms enrich the soil with their droppings and also tunnel through it making air passages.*

## Crop rotation

Crop rotation involves making sure that a single field is used for different things from season to season. For example, sheep may graze on a field one year, then wheat be grown on it the next, then hay the following year. Research shows that organic farming and crop rotation are good ways for farmers to increase their yields, providing more food to sell or for their families to eat.

*Different crops are sown in the fields each year. Each takes different nutrients from the soil.*

*Many farmers grow crops using organic methods, even though this often requires more work.*

# SAVE THE SEEDS!

Over huge expanses of time, thousands of species of animals and plants become extinct. Unfortunately, as people use up more and more of Earth's resources, more and more plants are becoming extinct. But plants are important to us. They are the major food source for animals, including humans. They also provide us with a whole host of products such as medicines, fuel for heating, lighting, and cooking, fibers for clothes, materials for building, and many other uses. Plants also help regulate the climate and protect the soil.

## In case of disaster . . .

Deep in a frozen mountain on the island of Svalbard in Norway, there is a vault - a huge concrete chamber which is actually a giant refrigerator full of seeds. The vault at Svalbard is just one of many seed banks around the world. Each one will eventually contain samples of all the seeds in the world's collections. If a disaster strikes, and plant life is wiped out, these hidden vaults could be opened and the seeds used to restock the land.

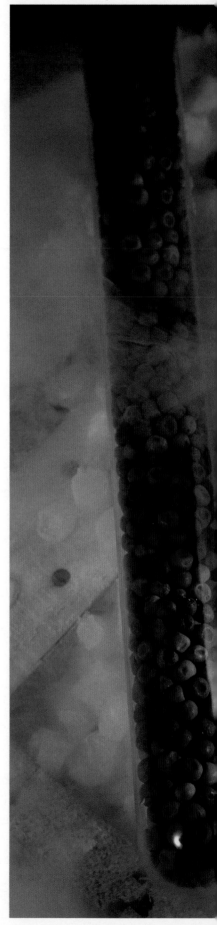

*Seeds are held in the vault at Svalbard frozen in ice.*

*Each batch of seeds is carefully labeled and stored at a cool temperature.*

## Millennium Seed Bank

A network of more than 50 countries is involved in the largest collection of all, the Millennium Seed Bank in the UK. Here around 14,000 types of seed are safely stored. They occupy little space, need very little attention and can be preserved, in the right conditions, almost indefinitely.

*Seeds are collected from plants all over the world and sent to the seed banks.*

# INSECT SWARMS

*A locust is a kind of grasshopper.*

## Locusts

Locusts normally live in the desert. This means that food is often hard to come by. To get around this, they move, or migrate, to different areas where they can find more to eat. A swarm of locusts can vary in size, but on average it contains around 50 million locusts. A swarm can measure 12 miles (20 km) long and stretch to 3 miles (5 km) wide. It can fly for up to 10 hours a day and cover 124 miles (200 km).

## Hungry bugs

A locust swarm has a huge appetite. It can munch through an average-sized field of crops in just two hours – or 11,000 tons (10,000 metric tons) of vegetation a day! That's enough to provide food for people for six to eight months. Locusts eat foods such as sorghum, beans, and millet, the crops many West African families eat. Locusts also eat the grass grown for animal feed, so the animals starve as well.

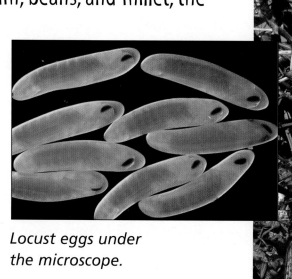

*Locust eggs under the microscope.*

After mating, the female locust lays an egg pod in the ground that contains 10–15 eggs. A tiny locust that has no wings, called a nymph, emerges from the egg and slowly grows into an adult locust.

*Locusts can strip all the leaves off a tree in minutes.*

*Dust is sprayed over a large area to catch the swarm before it flies.*

## Locust control

One way of controlling locusts in the past was to use insecticides on the vegetation to stop the nymphs from feeding. But these chemicals were found to be bad for the environment and were replaced by less dangerous ones.

A product called Green Muscle is based on a kind of fungus that infects the locust and kills it. It lasts for weeks, and is an environmentally friendly method of control.

# Pests and helpers

Bugs, creepy-crawlies, flies — all kinds of insects play a role in farming. Many are considered the farmers' enemies, others are the farmers' friends.

## Insect pests

Farmers must protect their crops from many kinds of insect pests that feed on the young plants. Some insects lay their eggs on the plant. Once these hatch, the young caterpillars and grubs grow and swell as they eat their way through whole fields.

The spotted cucumber beetle is an example. It infests a whole field, eating the leaves of crops such as cucumbers, soybeans, cotton, beans and many others. In the larval (caterpillar) form, it tunnels through the roots of young plants, stunting or killing them.

*Bollworm caterpillar eating a corncob.*

*Cabbage leaf covered in caterpillar pests.*

# Insect friends

Bees are good pollinators of plants. They collect pollen from flowers in a small pouch on their underside and carry it back to the hive. As they do so, they brush pollen from plant to plant, in this way fertilizing them.

Gardeners and farmers welcome these insects, but now, beekeepers around the world are worried about a parasite that is attacking bees, a mite called *Varroa destructor.* The bees become weakened by infections carried by *Varroa* and often become sick and die, or just too weak to fly.

As a result, across North America and Europe, the bees are failing to help pollinate crops. Indeed, if *Varroa* is not stopped, bees may be wiped out entirely in as little as ten years. Bees are also threatened by the poisonous insecticides being used to kill pests on crops.

*Colorado beetle larvae eat their way through plants.*

*Bees help to pollinate plants.*

# Killer chemicals

The problem with pesticides is that they can also affect humans. Sometimes spray drifts into the air we breathe; at other times, chemical residues remain on crops such as vegetables and fruit, and if we don't wash these thoroughly, we consume the chemicals when we eat the crop.

## Toxin-free food

We would all like to eat food that has no toxic substances, or poisons, in it at all. But it's unlikely we'll ever get rid of toxins altogether. According to tests, man-made toxins are found in almost all foods. In 2006, when 352 people were tested, all of them were found to have toxins in their blood. Most toxins are present in such small quantities they probably aren't dangerous. But scientists don't know what happens when these small amounts are mixed together.

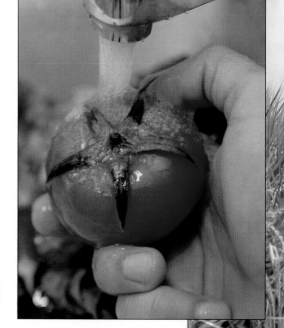

*It's wise to wash fruit and vegetables before eating.*

## Making us sick

Scientists believe that some chemicals that are used for pest control prevent brains from growing normally, especially in babies. They have also been blamed for other health problems, such as dizziness, sickness, headaches, and difficulties with breathing. Some chemicals are now banned in many countries, but they are still found in some foods – including butter, meat, fish, eggs, milk, olive oil, honey, orange juice, and brown bread.

*A farmer sprays pesticide onto a rice field.*

## Using pesticides

There are rules for using chemical pesticides that governments aim to enforce. Pesticides:

- should not harm animals or people
- should be easy and safe to store
- should be easy to handle
- should not leave a residue that stays long on or in plants, animals, water, soil, or crops

29

# TOO LITTLE, TOO MUCH

There's one big problem with farming. If farmers don't grow enough food, they don't make enough money to survive. However . . . if all the farmers produce lots of food, there's too much for sale and the price goes down so low that — once again — the farmers don't make enough money to survive.

## Subsidies

Many governments have tried to tackle this problem by guaranteeing farmers a fixed price for their produce so that there is always enough food being grown or produced. Unfortunately this creates a new problem when too much food is produced.

## Food mountains

In Europe, more than 14 million tons (13 million metric tons) of cereal, rice, sugar, and milk products are being stored in what are called "food mountains." One answer would be to give away this spare food to poorer countries. The problem then arises that the local farmers in Africa, Asia, and South America cannot sell their own produce and so they can't make enough money to survive.

*Corn continues to pour onto this mountain of surplus grain.*

# Wasting Food

Only 30–40 percent of the food produced in the U.S. and Europe ends up at the table, and it's a similar story in other rich countries around the world. Some of the food is lost while it's being transported from the farm to the market, some is not allowed to be sold because it doesn't meet government standards, and some goes bad. Also, people buy more food than they need and up to half of this is thrown away, sometimes without even being opened.

## Crooked carrots

For many years, some countries had laws about the size and shape of vegetables. No curly cucumbers, no crooked carrots, no small cauliflowers. Today the rules have been relaxed, but consumers have gotten used to buying vegetables for their looks – and not for their taste.

# ANIMAL WELFARE

Like all living things, humans are part of nature and depend on plants and other animals for survival. We are also conscious of ethical concerns – whether something is right or wrong. Most people, including farmers, generally believe that it is acceptable to use animals for food and other purposes, but that we must not abuse animals. We must avoid unnecessary suffering.

## INTENSIVE FARMERS BELIEVE:

... that they raise more productive and healthier animals than their parents or grandparents, and produce plenty of affordable, high-quality food.

... that modern housing protects the animals against bad weather, predators, accidental injuries, insects and parasites, and many diseases.

... that modern housing allows farmers to monitor animal health and provide proper nutrition, clean water, sanitation, and regular care.

... that they balance animal care with food safety and with environmental and cost considerations.

*Free-range hens live in a way that is more natural and free from stress.*

*Battery chickens are confined to small cages and have no freedom to move.*

# Right or wrong?

Buying food in our well-off societies is more complicated than ever before. Consumers, or shoppers, have to decide what's important to them. For example, free-range produce, from animals that live in more natural conditions with greater freedom and space, costs more than food that comes from animals that are farmed in large numbers and in cramped conditions.

# CRITICS BELIEVE:

... that modern intensive farming methods do not provide adequate living space, and that animals become stressed as a result.

... that being crowded together in large numbers is against the animals' natural instinct.

... that people are becoming more sensitive to the way food animals are raised.

... that people are willing to pay a higher price for food raised in systems that promote animal welfare.

... and some critics believe that the only way to ensure that animals are not treated cruelly is by not raising them for food and moving towards a meat-free diet.

# NEW FARMS, NEW FOODS

Farming isn't just about putting seeds in the ground and then harvesting the crop. There are many different kinds of modern food production, even without soil and even without a farm!

Most crops have traditional growing seasons. But these can be lengthened by farming in tunnels covered with transparent plastic sheeting. These are called polytunnels, and can be anywhere from 6½ to 23 feet (2 to 7 m) wide. Another way that growers extend the season is by covering their fields with thin polythene sheets called growing tunnels. The plastic retains both heat and moisture in the soil so that the seedlings develop quickly.

*Polytunnels are an economical form of greenhouse.*

## Hydroponics

Some fruit and vegetables can be grown successfully just using water to which key nutrients are added. The seeds may be supported in material such as sand or gravel, but other systems simply suspend the plants in water. Flowers grown by hydroponics provide a cash crop that can be shipped and sold around the world.

*These crops are being grown in water, without any soil at all.*

## Mycoprotein

Most processed foods start with crops that have been grown on farms, but Quorn is different. It is a high-protein, low-fat food that was developed 50 years ago in response to UN predictions of a world protein shortage. Its main ingredient is mycoprotein, which is made from a type of fungus, and produced in factories. It is fermented in 131-feet- (40-m-) high vats, spun into dough, and then cut up and frozen. The result is a food that's high in protein and fiber and low in fat.

# Farming in water

Today, most of the salt in the oceans comes from the continual rinsing of the soil and rocks by rainwater. Rain falling on the land dissolves the salts in the rocks, in a process known as chemical weathering – and these salts are washed into rivers and carried out to sea.

Most of the salt in the oceans and seas is sodium chloride, or ordinary table salt. This is also found in our bodies, and those of other animals, and it is essential for many life processes.

*A salt marsh*

*Sea lavender*

## Plants need salt

Plants do need some salts. These are called mineral salts. Plants get these iron and magnesium salts from the rock particles trapped in soil. The salts dissolve in rainwater and are then absorbed through the plant's roots. But sea salt is different; it damages the roots, and kills most plants.

## Salt water lovers

Some plants have found ways of coping with salty conditions. Scientists call these plants "halophytes." Many halophytes live in salt-water marshes that are covered in seawater at high tide.

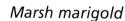

*Marsh marigold*

*Growing crops on a floating garden in Bangladesh.*

## Floating gardens

Land is scarce in Bangladesh and the situation is made worse by flooding which restricts the time that crops can be grown. Farmers here are creating floating gardens made of a raft of bamboo that rests on a bed of water-hyacinth plants. On top of this is a layer of soil in which seeds are planted. The nutrient-rich water keeps the plants fertilized. The floating gardens are used to grow leafy vegetables, and even rice.

*On the Inle Lake in Myanmar farmers use the same kind of techniques. Here tomato and rice crops are being cultivated on floating rafts.*

# WOMEN FARMERS

All over the world, women are taking an ever more important role in farming. They're doing this both to feed their families and to earn money from selling their crops.

In developing countries, one of the reasons this is happening is that many men are leaving the countryside to find work in the towns. They may stay away for whole weeks at a time, or even months. This leaves the day-to-day care of the family, the home and the land entirely in the women's hands.

## A cash start

Starting any new project requires investment, and there are many schemes that help women to improve the living conditions of their families and friends. The women are lent money, which they can use to buy goats, for example, and set up small businesses selling milk. They get free training, and are also taught how to read and write. Then these women can pass their learning on to people in other communities.

*Members of the Kenyan Women's Dairy Cooperative discuss receiving heifer cows.*

*A meeting of a women's cooperative in rural Bangladesh. The women are finding out how much money they've earned.*

# FAIRTRADE

Useful crops, such as coffee and tea, are known as commodities, and buying and selling them is big business across the world. Many commodities are produced by farmers in developing countries whose families live very hard lives, often in poverty. Because of this, buyers can purchase commodities at low prices, but the cost of growing these crops keeps rising. The result is that some farmers sell their crops for less money than it has taken to grow them.

The Fairtrade system is a network of organizations that want to trade in a fairer way. Fairtrade farmers are guaranteed a fair price, and agree to respect their environment by preventing soil erosion and protecting forests and rivers. Extra money is added to the price and used to help improve the farmers' lives.

*Coffee beans are harvested by hand.*

*The red berries on the coffee tree are ripe for picking.*

*Roasted beans ready for grinding.*

## Coffee

Coffee is grown in more than 50 countries around the world. Most coffee is grown near the equator, where the climate is right. The harvest begins when the red berries are picked from the bush. Each berry contains two seeds, or beans, which must be processed in one of two ways. Arabica beans are soaked and fermented. Then the flesh is removed and the beans are dried. Their papery skin is removed and they are graded for export. Robusta beans are usually sun-dried and then sold to a processing plant. Here the husks are removed and the beans are roasted and ground. Soluble coffee is made by grinding up beans, then freeze-drying them.

# HELPING HAND

To feed the world we need to grow and raise more food. We need a nutritious and healthy diet for everyone and we need to reduce the amount of food that we waste. Here are some of the things that you can do to ensure the planet doesn't go hungry in the future.

You can actually make a difference by making sure you eat the right kinds of foods and that these are the ones that your mom or dad buy, both for you and for the rest of the family.

## 1. Try something different

It takes 40 times as much water to produce 2.2 pounds (1 kg) of meat as it does to produce 2.2 pounds (1 kg) of vegetables. Go vegetarian once a week, support local growers and help save global resources.

## 2. Support Fairtrade

Look for the Fairtrade label on goods in stores as this guarantees that the overseas growers are getting a fair price for their produce.

## 3. Watch the food miles

Some food travels thousands of miles. Check what's grown locally or buy from local farms and market stalls.

## 4. Animal welfare

Look for a free-range or similar label on poultry (and eggs) to show that the chickens have been raised in healthy conditions and not in crowded sheds.

## 5. Don't over-shop

Buy only what you need – and eat what's in the fridge!

### Give a goat – or even a camel!

Many charities have schemes through which you can give seeds, equipment or an animal to a farming community in one of the developing countries. The international organization Oxfam Unwrapped has a Web site to tell you more.

### Change your diet

Rising world living standards are creating an increase in demand for protein-heavy foods and forcing prices up. This is encouraging people to select healthier foods that are rich in fiber, particularly fruit and vegetables.

### Grow your own

Growing your own vegetables is the best step to healthy eating – and it's lots of fun. Gardening isn't just for people with lots of land. Seed packet instructions, books and Web sites are all available to help you raise your own crops.

# GLOSSARY

**animal welfare** A policy of treating all animals in a humane way so that they do not suffer unnecessarily.

**arabica** A species of coffee plant, generally considered the best (the other is robusta).

**arable (land)** Land suitable for growing crops.

**arid** Dry, lacking sufficient water or rainfall.

**atmosphere** A blanket of gases that surrounds a planet, a moon or a star, including Earth.

**bacteria** One-celled organisms found in rotting matter, in air, in soil, and in living bodies.

**battery chicken** A chicken raised in a cage to produce eggs and meat.

**cash crop** A crop that is grown and sold for cash in the open market.

**caterpillar** The larva state of a butterfly or moth.

**cholesterol** A type of fat that is found in some of the foods we eat.

**coffee** The beans of this tropical plant are roasted and ground to make a drink.

**commodity** A crop or goods available from a variety of producers.

**compost** The decomposed remains of plants and animals that can be used to fertilize soil, and improve its structure and its ability to hold water.

**crop** The season's yield of any plant that is grown to be harvested as food or for any other economic purpose.

**crop rotation** The use of the same land to grow different crops in successive seasons.

**crop-spraying / crop-dusting** Applying pesticides or fertilizers by spray, often from a small aircraft.

**deforestation** The destruction of natural forest land for cropland, pasture, or human settlement.

**desert** An arid landscape that receives little rain and has very little vegetation.

**desertification** The spread of an established desert into the surrounding area, caused both by reduced rainfall and by human factors such as overgrazing of farm animals or overusing water resources.

**erosion** The process in which Earth's surface is worn away by water and/or wind.

**Fairtrade** An international network of organizations that help producers in developing countries to improve their farming methods and get fair prices for their crops.

**fertilizer** Any substance that is used to make soil more fertile, such as manure or a mixture of chemicals.

**floating garden** A floating platform used for growing vegetables and fruits.

**food mountain** Popular term for the surplus food produced as the result of subsidizing farmers to grow more food than is needed locally.

**free-range chicken** A chicken allowed to roam freely instead of being kept in a confined space.

**fungus** Spore-producing organism such as yeasts, molds, and mushrooms.

**gene** A unit within the cellular makeup of a living being that holds certain information to build and maintain aspects of that organism's cells and to pass genetic traits to offspring.

**genetic modification (GM)** The alteration of cells or organisms at a genetic (cell) level in order to turn them into new substances or enable them to perform new functions.

**Great Green Wall** Huge planting projects to create green belts of trees and vegetation to halt the spread of desert, one across China and another across Africa.

**Greenpeace** An international campaigning organization working for environmental conservation.

**Green Revolution** The transformation of agriculture, especially in the Indian subcontinent, through the introduction of pesticides, high-yield grains, and better management.

**growing tunnel** A low structure of polythene sheet on a wire frame to accelerate the germination and early growth of crops in the field.

**halophyte** A plant that grows naturally in salty soil.

**humus**   Partially decomposed organic matter which forms the organic component of soil.

**hydroponics**   A method of cultivating plants without soil in water containing chemical nutrients.

**inorganic**   Composed of material that is neither plant nor animal in origin.

**insecticide**   A chemical pesticide formulated to kill insects.

**larva**   A stage of growth for some insects, after hatching from the egg and before full adulthood (plural: larvae).

**locust**   A kind of large grasshopper that flies in swarms and eats crops and other vegetation.

**manure**   Animal dung used to fertilize land and crops.

**migration**   The regular seasonal journey undertaken by many creatures, including birds, fish and mammals.

**Millennium Seed Bank**   A collection of around 14,000 types of seed of threatened plant species from around the world stored in the UK to preserve them for the future.

**mold**   Fungus that grows on various kinds of damp or decaying organic matter.

**mycoprotein**   A nutritious food product made from a kind of fungus.

**nutrient**   A substance that provides food or nourishment.

**organic farming**   A method of farming that minimizes the use of chemicals in the production process.

**organism**   A complete living thing, such as animal, plant, fungus, or microorganism.

**overgrazing**   Grazing livestock intensively, to the point at which the land becomes damaged.

**parasite**   An animal that lives in or on another animal and obtains nourishment from it without killing it.

**pest**   A destructive insect or other animal that attacks food, crops, or livestock.

**pest control**   The control of a species that is defined as a pest.

**pesticide**   A substance intended for preventing, destroying or repelling any pest.

**pollen**   A fine powder made by the male elements of flowers, and generally carried by bees from flower to flower as part of the fertilization process.

**polytunnel**   A steel-framed walk-in structure covered with plastic sheeting used to lengthen the growing season for many kinds of crops.

**Quorn**   A high-protein processed food based on mycoprotein.

**robusta**   A species of coffee plant, considered not to have as good a flavor as arabica.

**subsidy**   Financial assistance paid to farmers (or others) to help them with their business.

**sustainable**   In farming, able to continue to be productive without causing damage to the environment or to natural resources.

**topsoil**   The upper layer of soil, which generally has the highest concentration of organic matter and is the most fertile.

**toxin**   A poisonous substance produced by a living organism.

**UN (United Nations)**   An organization of independent states formed in 1945 to promote international peace and security.

**volcanic eruption**   The explosion of a volcano, discharging ash, gas and rock.

**windbreak**   A barrier of trees and shrubs, or any other structure that is designed to protect an area from effects of wind.

# INDEX

# PHOTO CREDITS

(t=top, b=bottom, l=left, r=right)